America's Game
Pittsburgh Pirates

CHRIS W. SEHNERT

ABDO & Daughters
PUBLISHING

Published by Abdo & Daughters, 4940 Viking Dr., Suite 622, Edina, MN 55435.

Cover photo: Allsport
Interior photos: Archive Photos, pages 5, 10, 11, 21, 28
                    Wide World Photo: pages 9, 15-17, 22, 23, 25-27

Edited by Paul Joseph

Library of Congress Cataloging–in–Publication Data
Sehnert, Chris W.
      The Pittsburgh Pirates / Chris W. Sehnert
           p. cm. — (America's game)
      Includes index.
      Summary: Focuses on some of the key players in the history of the team that has been playing professional baseball in Pittsburgh for more than 100 years.
      ISBN   1-56239-660-9
      1. Pittsburgh Pirates (Baseball team)—History—Juvenile literature. [1. Pittsburgh Pirates (Baseball team)—History.
2. Baseball—History.] I. Title. II. Series.
GV875.P5S45   1997
796.357'64'0974886—dc20   96-1514
                                                              CIP
                                                              AC

Contents

The Pittsburgh Pirates

The Pittsburgh Pirates are one of professional baseball's oldest teams. Originally named the Alleghenys for their regional location, they later became the Pirates. The Modern Era of Major League Baseball was kicked off when the Pirates met the Boston Pilgrims in the first World Series in 1903. Through the years, the Pirates have won nine National League (NL) Pennants and five World Championships.

From Honus Wagner to Barry Bonds, some of the greatest players in baseball history have worn the Pirate uniform. Paul and Lloyd Waner took the NL by storm in the 1920s, becoming baseball's most potent brotherly combination. Two decades later, Ralph Kiner would begin a string of seven straight home run crowns.

Bill Mazeroski, known for his glove, became a household word when his homer ended the 1960 World Series. In the outfield that season was a young Puerto Rican named Roberto Clemente. On the field, Clemente was among the best that ever played.

In the 1970s, the Pirates were led by their Hall of Famer, Willie "Pops" Stargell. Their 1979 World Championship left fans cheering from coast to coast.

Today the Pirates' ship stays afloat on the rocky waters of big business. While unions and executives continue to battle, the game itself still remains the same.

Players like Denny Naegle, Orlando Merced and Midre Cummings are continuing to search for the next Pirate pennant.

Pittsburgh Pirates' Barry Bonds hits a solo homer in Game 6 of the 1992 National League Championship Series against the Atlanta Braves.

The Pittsburgh Alleghenys

Major League Baseball is tied to its past through historic organizations. A handful of these clubs remain today, more than a century after professional baseball began.

The Pittsburgh Pirates' organization dates back to 1882. That year, Pittsburgh's Alleghenys, previously a minor league baseball club, became charter members of the new American Association (AA). In the years to come, the Alleghenys would change leagues as well as their name.

American Association

The AA was formed as a rival to the older NL, which was established in 1876. The Alleghenys played five seasons in the AA. In 1887, Pittsburgh became the first member of the AA to jump to the more established NL.

The AA folded after the 1891 season. The National League remains today as baseball's "Senior Circuit." The newer American League (AL) would join the major league ranks in 1900.

A plaque honoring James Galvin in the Baseball Hall of Fame at Cooperstown, New York.

James Galvin

The Alleghenys of the late 1880s were led by the pitching of James Galvin. "The Little Steam Engine," as he was also known, joined Pittsburgh's team in 1885.

Galvin was a small man at 5 feet, 8 inches tall. He led the NL in shutouts in 1883 and 1884, while pitching for the Buffalo Bisons. He is the only man in major league history credited with pitching *two* perfect games! With the Alleghenys, he won 103 games in his first four seasons.

His career ended in 1892 with 360 career victories. He ranks second on the all-time list, behind Cy Young, for complete games with 639. Galvin was inducted into the Baseball Hall of Fame in 1965.

Name Change

In 1890, Pittsburgh's NL team changed its name to the Innocents. It was the worst season in club history. They finished 66 games out of first place with a record of 23-113. Needing a change, Pittsburgh's baseball club changed its name to the Pirates in 1892.

The Flying Dutchman

Honus Wagner is widely revered as the greatest shortstop to ever play the game of baseball. "The Flying Dutchman," as he was called, stood 5 feet, 11 inches tall, and weighed 200 pounds. He was bowlegged, and fast.

Honus won the NL batting title eight times. He led the NL in stolen bases and runs batted in (RBIs) five times. When he retired in 1917, he was the NL's career leader in hits, runs, singles, doubles, and triples!

John Peter "Honus" Wagner became one of five inaugural inductees into the Baseball Hall of Fame in 1936. The four others were Babe Ruth, Ty Cobb, Walter Johnson, and Christy Mathewson.

Left: Honus Wagner of the Pittsburgh Pirates, in a photo taken in 1915.
Facing Page: At left, the Dodgers' Max Carey; center and right, the Pirates' Honus Wagner and George Gibson.

Pirates Meet Pilgrims

The Pirates began a three-year string of NL domination in 1901. They won their first pennant that year by 7.5 games over the Philadelphia Phillies.

The following year, Pittsburgh put together the best season in franchise history (103-36). They finished the 1902 season 27.5 games in front of second-place Brooklyn. It remains the largest margin of victory in major league history.

The Pirates' Ginger Beaumont, Tommy Leach, and Honus Wagner combined to lead the NL in nearly every offensive category. Pitcher Jack Chesbro led the league in wins (28) and shutouts (8).

The 1903 Pirates won their third-straight NL Pennant by 6.5 games over the New York Giants. Wagner won the NL batting crown (.355), and Player-Manager Fred Clarke finished second (.351). Pitcher Sam Leever led the NL in earned run average (ERA) and wins.

After the 1903 season, Pittsburgh owner Barney Dreyfuss challenged the AL Champion Boston to a best-of-nine World Championship. The Pirates lost the series in eight games. Leever was injured and unable to pitch. Deacon Phillippe pitched five complete games for Pittsburgh, accounting for all three of their victories. Cy Young and Bill Dinneen led Boston as the upstart AL won the first modern day World Series.

A Classic Matchup

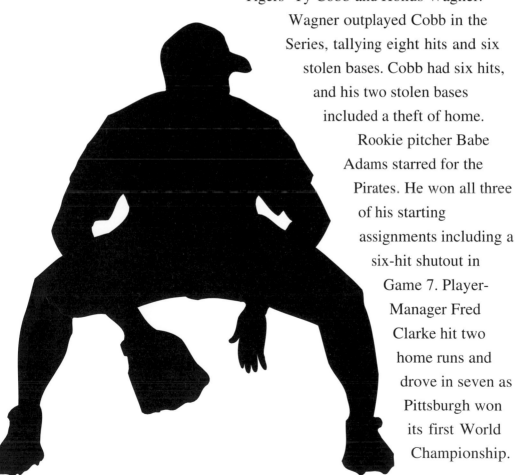

The Pirates moved into historic Forbes Field and returned to the World Series in 1909. They faced the AL Champion Detroit Tigers. It was a classic matchup between two of the game's finest hitters, the Tigers' Ty Cobb and Honus Wagner. Wagner outplayed Cobb in the Series, tallying eight hits and six stolen bases. Cobb had six hits, and his two stolen bases included a theft of home. Rookie pitcher Babe Adams starred for the Pirates. He won all three of his starting assignments including a six-hit shutout in Game 7. Player-Manager Fred Clarke hit two home runs and drove in seven as Pittsburgh won its first World Championship.

Pirate Pie

Harold "Pie" Traynor joined the Pirates in 1920. He soon became a fixture at third base. The Pie Man (whose favorite dessert was well known) was a defensive wizard.

With Traynor holding down the hot corner, the Pirates returned to the World Series in 1925. Their opponents were the defending World Champion Washington Senators, led by the great Walter Johnson.

Pie Traynor led all NL third basemen that same year with a .957 Fielding Average.

The Pirates lost Game 1 of the 1925 World Series (4-1) when Walter Johnson threw a 5-hitter. Traynor's solo-homer accounted for Pittsburgh's only run.

Johnson's six-hit shutout in Game 4 gave the Senators a commanding 3-1 series lead. It was the last World Series victory in his amazing career.

With their backs against the wall, the Bucs came back to win the next two games and tie the Series. In Game 7, Pittsburgh finally got to Johnson. They came from four runs down to defeat the Senators 9-7, and win their second World Championship!

Pie Traynor played his entire 18-year career with the Pirates. He took over as player-manager in 1934, and remained as manager for two seasons after his playing career ended. He holds the NL record for lifetime putouts by a third baseman (2,288). Harold "Pie" Traynor was inducted into the Baseball Hall of Fame in 1948.

Facing Page: Harold "Pie" Traynor, Hall-of-Fame third baseman of the Pittsburgh Pirates.

The Waner Brothers

Paul Waner joined Pittsburgh in 1926. He won the NL batting crown (.336) in his rookie season. Lloyd Waner arrived the following year. Together with Pie Traynor, the Waners carried the Pirates to another NL Pennant in 1927.

Lloyd played centerfield and batted lead-off. Paul was in right field and batted third in the order. In Lloyd's rookie season (1927), he led the NL in runs (133), while Paul led in hits (237), triples (18), RBIs (131), and took his second NL batting crown in a row (.380).

The Pirates edged the St. Louis Cardinals in the 1927 NL pennant race by 1.5 games. They faced the New York Yankees in the World Series.

The 1927 Yankees were led by Babe Ruth and Lou Gehrig. They are considered to be one of the best teams that ever played the game. The Waner brothers out-hit New York's fearsome tandem in the 1927 World Series, but the Pirates were swept in four games.

The Waners never returned to the post-season. They both retired in 1945, combining for more hits (5,611) than any other brotherly combination in major league history.

Facing page: Lloyd Waner at the plate.
Above: Paul Waner makes a leaping catch.

17

Pittsburgh

When he retired in 1917, Honus Wagner was the NL's career leader in hits, runs, singles, doubles, and triples.

Harold "Pie" Traynor holds the NL record for lifetime putouts by a third baseman (2,288).

In Lloyd Waner's rookie season, 1927, he led the NL with 133 runs.

Ralph Kiner became a member of the Hall of Fame in 1975.

Pirates

Barry Bonds won the first of his three NL MVP Awards in 1990.

On September 30, 1972, baseball great Roberto Clemente doubled in the final regular season game of his career. It was hit number 3,000.

Orlando Merced is one of several young players the Pirates hope will rebuild the team.

Bill Mazeroski won the Gold Glove Award 8 times in his 17-year career.

Vaughan and Kiner

Pittsburgh fans waited more than three decades for their baseball team to make it back to the World Series. In the meantime, two star players gave them much to cheer about.

Joseph Floyd Vaughan came to the Pirates in 1932. He made the first of his nine-straight All-Star appearances in 1934. He won an NL batting crown in 1935 (.385) with the greatest hitting performance by a shortstop since Honus Wagner. It remains the second-highest batting average for an NL shortstop to this day.

Vaughan's life ended tragically in a boating accident in 1952. He was 40 years old. Vaughan was inducted into the Baseball Hall of Fame in 1985.

Ralph Kiner's first season in the majors was 1946. He started with a bang. Twenty-three bangs to be exact. That was his home run total in his rookie season, and it led the NL.

Kiner went on to lead the NL in homers every year until 1952. His finest season came in 1949 when he led the NL in home runs (54), RBIs (127), walks (117), and slugging percentage (.658).

The Pirates finished on the bottom of the NL in 1952. The next year, after seven-straight NL home run titles, Kiner was traded to the the Chicago Cubs. He retired at the age of 32 because of severe back pain. Ralph Kiner became a member of the Hall of Fame in 1975.

Facing Page: Ralph Kiner, Hall-of-Fame slugger for the Pittsburgh Pirates.

Maz

The Pirates finished last in the NL five times between 1950 and 1955. They rose from the depths to finish second in 1958. In 1960, Pittsburgh won the NL Pennant for the first time in 33 years. The Bucs received All-Star performances from three veteran pitchers in 1960. Vern Law won the Cy Young Award with 20 wins and 18 complete games. Bob Friend picked up 18 wins, and Elroy Face finished second in the NL with 24 saves.

The staff was backed up by the league's top-ranked defense. Shortstop Dick Groat won the NL's batting crown (.325) and MVP honors. Bill Mazeroski led all NL second basemen in fielding average (.989), and won his second Gold Glove. The outfield included future 12-time Gold Glove winner, Roberto Clemente.

The Gold Glove Award was first introduced in 1957 as a way of rewarding the top defensive player at each position. Mazeroski received the award 8 times in his 17-year career.

It was Mazeroski's bat that put an end to the 1960 baseball season, however. The New York Yankees were heavily favored to beat Pittsburgh in the World Series. Their power-laden lineup included Mickey Mantle, Roger Maris, Yogi Berra, and the dominant pitching of Whitey Ford.

The Yankees outscored the Pirates 46-17 through six games, but the Series was tied at three games apiece! Game 7 was tied (9-9) when Mazeroski stepped up to the plate in the bottom of the ninth inning.

Mazeroski smashed a drive over the left field wall. Pittsburgh fans went wild. The Pirates became World Champions for the third time.

Roberto And Willie

Pittsburgh remained a talented team in the 1960s. Two of their star players were Roberto Clemente and Willie Stargell. Roberto Clemente was from Puerto Rico. He played his first major league game for the Pittsburgh Pirates in 1955. Clemente was joined in Pittsburgh's outfield by a power-hitting left-hander named Wilver "Willie" Stargell in 1962. Stargell went on to play 21 seasons with the Pirates.

The major leagues expanded to 24 teams in 1969, and split each league into two divisions. The Pirates began the new decade by moving into Three Rivers Stadium, and proceeded to win the NL's Eastern Division six times in the 1970s.

Roberto Clemente makes a sensational backhanded grab in right-center field, catching a long drive by Bobby Thomson of the Chicago Cubs.

In 1970 and 1972, Pittsburgh was beaten in the National League Championship Series (NLCS) by the "Big Red Machine" of Cincinnati. In between, the Pirates defeated the San Francisco Giants to capture the 1971 NL Pennant.

The Pirates played the Baltimore Orioles in the 1971 World Series. It was Baltimore's third World Series appearance in a row.

The Pirates defeated Baltimore in seven games to become World Champions for the fourth time. Roberto Clemente's solo homer lifted Pittsburgh to a 2-1 victory in the final game.

On September 30, 1972, Clemente doubled in the final regular season game of his career. It was hit number 3,000.

Each season the Baseball Hall of Fame awards a single major league player for outstanding citizenship. It's called the Roberto Clemente Award. Roberto Clemente died on December 31, 1972, when the plane in which he was traveling crashed into the ocean. Clemente was leading a relief effort for people left homeless by a devastating earthquake in Nicaragua. It was not an unusual occasion for a man who once said, "If you have an opportunity to make things better and you don't, then you are wasting your time on this earth."

Immediately following his tragic death, Roberto Clemente was inducted into the Baseball Hall of Fame.

Clemente won four batting crowns. He holds the NL record for most years leading the league in outfield assists, with five. He once threw a runner out at the plate on what should have been a bases-loaded single. He was the NL MVP in 1966 and the World Series MVP in 1971.

Pittsburgh won the NL East again in 1974 and 1975. Both times they were defeated in the NLCS. They finished the decade with one more Eastern Division Title in 1979.

Willie Stargell finished second or third in NL MVP voting three times in the early 1970s. He won his first home run crown (48) in 1971. In 1973, he led the NL in doubles (43), HRs (44), RBIs (119), and slugging percentage (.646). He saved his most memorable performance for 1979.

At the age of 39, Stargell was referred to by his teammates as "Pops." As team captain, he rewarded players who made outstanding efforts on the field with a gold "Stargell Star." The team became united behind Willie's leadership.

Stargell, now a full-time first baseman, had the league's best fielding average (.997). His role in bringing the Pirates to another division championship earned him the NL's MVP honor.

The Pirates swept the Cincinnati Reds (3-0) in the playoffs. Stargell was *on fire!* He pounded out 5 hits in 11 trips to the plate, including two homers and a pair of doubles. He was named MVP of the 1979 NLCS.

Pittsburgh lost three of the first four games to the Baltimore Orioles in the 1979 World Series. They came back to tie the Series (3-3) with solid pitching from Bert Blyleven, John Candelaria, and the submarine style relief of Kent Tekulve.

In Game 7, Stargell took over. He went 4-for-5 with 2 doubles and a 2-run home run. It was all the Pirates needed to defeat the Orioles (4-1) and win their fifth World Championship.

Willie Stargell was named the MVP of the 1979 World Series (.400 batting average, 3 HRs, and 7 RBIs). It was his third MVP Award of the year! He retired after the 1982 season, and was inducted into the Baseball Hall of Fame in 1988.

Right: Willie Stargell.

The 1990s

The Pirates did not return to NLCS in the 1980s. They won their first of three-straight Eastern Division Titles in 1990, thanks to some young, talented players.

Barry Bonds was the best of the talent, and the son of Bobby Bonds, an All-Star outfielder. Barry's godfather is Hall-of-Fame outfielder Willie Mays. Barry came to the major leagues in 1986, and began to live up to the family tradition.

Bonds won the first of his three NL MVP Awards in 1990. He combined outstanding offensive statistics (.301 batting average, 33 HRs, 114 RBIs, and 52 stolen bases) with his first Gold Glove performance as Pittsburgh's left fielder.

Joining Bonds in the Pirate outfield were Bobby Bonilla and the NL's Gold Glove center fielder, Andy Van Slyke. Bonilla finished second to Bonds in the 1990 NL MVP voting. Doug Drabek led the NL in wins (22), and won the league's Cy Young Award.

Pittsburgh was defeated in the 1990 NLCS by the Cincinnati Reds. They won the Eastern Division again in 1991 and 1992. John Smiley led the NL in wins (20) in 1991. And in 1992, Bonds won his second MVP Award. The Atlanta Braves defeated Pittsburgh in the NLCS both times.

Facing page: Bobby Bonilla hits a home run against the Chicago Cubs.
Right: Barry Bonds slides into home on a double steal against the New York Mets.

Troubled Waters

The age of player free agency has been hard on Pittsburgh baseball fans. The Pirates have had difficulty maintaining the salary demands of their star players. Bonds, Bonilla, Smiley, and Drabek all left Pittsburgh before the 1993 season.

The Pirates transferred to the new NL Central Division in 1994. They finished 1995 with the worst record in the NL (58-86). The Pirate organization was sold after the season.

The new ownership will keep the team in Pittsburgh, and try to rebuild the franchise. Young players like Orlando Merced, Denny Naegle and Midre Cummings will be looked to for leadership.

The Pittsburgh Pirates' organization has been playing Major League Baseball for over 100 years. They have produced nine NL Pennant winners and five World Championship teams. They have faced rough times in the past, but the Pirates' ship, with its great tradition of players, will continue to sail onward!

Orlando Merced slides home safely in a game against the Atlanta Braves.

Glossary

All-Star: A player who is voted by fans as the best player at one position in a given year.

American League (AL): An association of baseball teams formed in 1900 which make up one-half of the major leagues.

American League Championship Series (ALCS): A best-of-seven-game playoff with the winner going to the World Series to face the National League Champions.

Batting Average: A baseball statistic calculated by dividing a batter's hits by the number of times at bat.

Earned Run Average (ERA): A baseball statistic which calculates the average number of runs a pitcher gives up per nine innings of work.

Fielding Average: A baseball statistic which calculates a fielder's success rate based on the number of chances the player has to record an out.

Hall of Fame: A memorial for the greatest baseball players of all time located in Cooperstown, New York.

Home Run (HR): A play in baseball where a batter hits the ball over the outfield fence scoring everyone on base as well as the batter.

Major Leagues: The highest ranking associations of professional baseball teams in the world, currently consisting of the American and National Baseball Leagues.

Minor Leagues: A system of professional baseball leagues at levels below Major League Baseball.

National League (NL): An association of baseball teams formed in 1876 which make up one-half of the major leagues.

National League Championship Series (NLCS): A best-of-seven-game playoff with the winner going to the World Series to face the American League Champions.

Pennant: A flag which symbolizes the championship of a professional baseball league.

Pitcher: The player on a baseball team who throws the ball for the batter to hit. The pitcher stands on a mound and pitches the ball toward the strike zone area above the plate.

Plate: The place on a baseball field where a player stands to bat. It is used to determine the width of the strike zone. Forming the point of the diamond-shaped field, it is the final goal a base runner must reach to score a run.

RBI: A baseball statistic standing for *runs batted in.* Players receive an RBI for each run that scores on their hits.

Rookie: A first-year player, especially in a professional sport.

Slugging Percentage: A statistic which points out a player's ability to hit for extra bases by taking the number of total bases hit and dividing it by the number of at bats.

Stolen Base: A play in baseball when a base runner advances to the next base while the pitcher is delivering his pitch.

Strikeout: A play in baseball when a batter is called out for failing to put the ball in play after the pitcher has delivered three strikes.

Triple Crown: A rare accomplishment when a single player finishes a season leading their league in batting average, home runs, and RBIs. A pitcher can win a Triple Crown by leading the league in wins, ERA, and strikeouts.

Walk: A play in baseball when a batter receives four pitches out of the strike zone and is allowed to go to first base.

World Series: The championship of Major League Baseball played since 1903 between the pennant winners from the American and National Leagues.

Index